Enemies all around

Story by Penny Frank

Illustrated by Tony Morris

THE LION
STORY BIBLE

24

TRING · BATAVIA · SYDNEY

The Bible tells us
how God chose the nation of Israel to
be his special people. He made them a
promise that he would always love
and care for them. But they must
obey him.
This is the story of King Hezekiah,
who trusted God when there were
powerful enemies all around. You can
find this story in your own Bible, in
the second book of Kings, chapters 18
to 20.

Copyright © 1986 Lion Publishing

Published by
Lion Publishing plc
Icknield Way, Tring, Herts, England
ISBN 0 85648 737 6
Lion Publishing Corporation
1705 Hubbard Avenue, Batavia
Illinois 60510. USA
ISBN 0 85648 737 6
Albatross Books Pty Ltd
PO Box 320, Sutherland. NSW 2232. Australia
ISBN 0 86760 521 9

First edition 1986

British Library Cataloguing in Publication Data
Frank, Penny
Enemies all around. – (The Lion
Story Bible; v.24)
1. Hezekiah – Juvenile literature
2. Bible stories, English – O.T. Kings,
2nd
I. Title   II. Morris, Tony, *1938
Aug 2 -*
222'.540924   BS580.H4
ISBN 0-85648-749-X

Library of Congress Cataloging-in-Publication Data
Frank, Penny.
Enemies all around.
(The Lion Story Bible; 24)
1. Hezekiah, King of Judah—Juvenile
literature. [1. Hezekiah, King of Judah.
2. Bible stories—O.T.] I. Morris, Tony,
ill. II. Title. III. Series: Frank, Penny.
Lion Story Bible; 24.
BS580.H4F73 1986   222'.5409505
85-23865
ISBN 0-85648-749-X

God's people were glad. They had a
good king to rule them. His name was
Hezekiah.

King Hezekiah obeyed God and asked
for God's help in everything he did.

It was a good thing he did, because God's people faced a deadly enemy in those days. His name was Sennacherib, king of Assyria.

Everyone had heard of Sennacherib. He
was so powerful and cruel that people
talked about him in whispers.

'He burns down whole cities, you
know,' they told each other. 'His soldiers
are so well-armed, they win every battle
they fight.'

One day, the people in Jerusalem heard that Sennacherib's army was coming. Soldiers were marching towards the city.

They shut and barred the gates. The city
walls of Jerusalem were strong and high.
Each day King Hezekiah and his people
looked out from the walls to see if the
army was near. They knew Sennacherib
was fighting the other towns on the way.

The day came when the great army of Sennacherib arrived at the gates of Jerusalem. The sun shone on their sharp spears.

The city was surrounded. All the people were trapped inside.

Sennacherib sent a messenger to the city gate.

'You'd better come and talk to me, Hezekiah,' he shouted. 'I have an important message for you.'

King Hezekiah sent out his three
advisers to talk to Sennacherib's
messenger.

The messenger said, 'Why don't you
give up now? You know that we are
stronger than you.

'Don't tell me that Hezekiah is
trusting in his God. That would really
make me laugh.'

The people on the city wall could hear
all that the messenger was saying.

'Don't let King Hezekiah fool you,' he
shouted up to them. 'You'll never win a
battle against Sennacherib. No one else
has. Hezekiah is telling you lies.'

'What makes you think your God is so much better than the gods of other lands?' the messenger went on. 'We won against them. We shall win against you.

'Don't fool yourselves that your God will save you.'

But the people did not answer. King Hezekiah had told them not to say a word!

The three advisers went back to King
Hezekiah and told him all that
Sennacherib's messenger had said.
    King Hezekiah was very worried.

He sent his servant with a message to the prophet Isaiah.

'King Sennacherib's messenger has insulted the living God. Pray to God for us.'

God had chosen Isaiah to be his prophet. God talked to him about everything that happened. Isaiah told the people what God said.

Isaiah listened to the king's message.
'Don't be frightened by what Sennacherib says,' he answered. 'God will send the Assyrians back home.'

But just then a man came from Sennacherib with a letter. It said, 'You seem to think your God is big enough to fight me. I know he is not. He will never beat me.'

When King Hezekiah had read the letter he took it to God's temple. He unrolled the letter.

'You are the only true God. You rule the world,' Hezekiah said to God. 'Just look at what Sennacherib says. He thinks you are a god made of wood or stone like the gods of other nations.

'Please protect your people and show Sennacherib that you are the only living God.'

God answered the king's prayer. Isaiah sent him a message for Sennacherib and his army.

'We are all laughing at you in Jerusalem,' the message said.

'You think our God will not be able to stop you when you fight us. But he knew that you were coming. He is ready for the battle. He says he will not even let you come into the city.'

The next morning the Israelites peeped over the city wall to see what was happening. They could hardly believe their eyes.

Every soldier who had come to fight them was dead, and they could see King Sennacherib galloping away over the hills, as fast as his horse could go.

God had kept his promise. The army had not even been into the city. Now there was peace in Jerusalem.

The Lion Story Bible is made up of 52 individual stories for young readers, building up an understanding of the Bible as one story — God's story — a story for all time and all people.

The Old Testament section (numbers 1–30) tells the story of a great nation — God's chosen people, the Israelites — and God's love and care for them through good times and bad. The stories are about people who knew and trusted God. From this nation came one special person, Jesus Christ, sent by God to save all people everywhere.

The story of *Enemies all around* comes from the Old Testament history book, 2 Kings, chapters 18–20. It is also told in Isaiah, chapters 36–38.

Hezekiah is king of the tiny southern kingdom of Judah. Just a few years earlier, the larger northern kingdom of Israel had fallen to the invading Assyrians because they had ignored God's repeated warnings.

No wonder King Hezekiah and his people were scared when the Assyrian army came hammering at the gates! Country after country had fallen to these fierce fighters. Could anything save Judah? No.

But *someone* could. God is always in control of his world. He always listens when his people call to him for help. If they are ready to trust him no army on earth can defeat them.

In the crisis, Hezekiah put his whole trust in God, and the nation was saved.

The next story in this series, number 25: *Jeremiah and the great disaster*, tells what happened when God's people failed to trust him.